Brand Pov V

"Ask 100 people to define "brand" and you'll get 100 different answers, but Walker deconstructs the mythology and the confusion into smart, translatable business ideas that focus on what matters most: results. In a world where, increasingly, commoditization is becoming the rule rather than the exception, Walker provides a playbook for creating differentiation and shaping brands that resonate with associates, partners, and customers. This is a must-have tome for anyone wanting a more facile understanding of how to stand out in a cluttered marketplace."

Chas Withers, president and chief operating officer
Dix & Eaton

"Brand Power for Small Business Entrepreneurs is just that—power! Walker decodes big business branding strategies using a no-nonsense approach that will give your small business the leverage it needs to successfully communicate and execute your brand. A must-read for every small business owner that wants to successfully communicate their value to customers to maintain a competitive advantage in the marketplace."

Deborah Gray, Ph.D., faculty
College of Business Administration
Central Michigan University

"Brand Power for Small Business Entrepreneurs is the one book that entrepreneurs need to read this year and then again every year. In fact, leaders at big companies should read this, too. Brand

Power is one of the most compelling books I have ever read—not just about the importance of marketing and communications to your success but how to harness both to ensure that success. The chapter on goals and strategies offers an excellent approach that business leaders should read again and again. And Renee Walker also has created the absolute practical primer on how to network for success. Everyone networks, but how often does it really help grow your business? It will now, after you read this excellent book!"

Gary Wells, senior managing director
Dix & Eaton

"Walker's laser-focused ability to create successful strategies is the foundation of this blueprint for entrepreneurs. Brand Power for Small Business Entrepreneurs combines her extensive experience with practical solutions to drive growth."

Leslie Backus, APR, president
Leslie J. Backus, Inc.

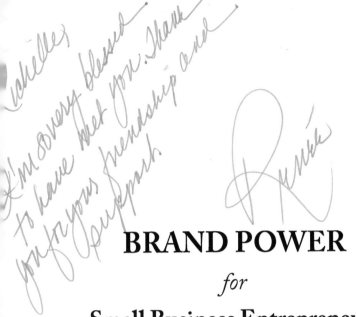

BRAND POWER

for

Small Business Entrepreneurs

*Breakout Brand, Positioning, and Profit Strategies
to Drive Revenue Growth*

RENÉE T. WALKER

Published by RENEE WALKER & ASSOCIATES LLC, West Bloom-field, Michigan.

No part of this publication may be reproduced, stored in a retrieval system, or transmitted in any form or by any means, electronic, mechanical, photocopying, recording, scanning, or otherwise, except as permitted under Section 107 or 108 of the 1976 United States Copyright Act, without either the prior written permission of the publisher, or authorization through payment of the appropriate per-copy fee to the Copyright Clearance Center, Inc., 222 Rosewood Drive, Danvers, MA 01923, (978) 750-8400 phone, (978) 646-8600 fax, or on the web at www.copyright.com. Requests to the publisher for permission should be addressed to the Permissions Department, RENEE WALKER & ASSOCIATES LLC, 6689 Orchard Lake Road #134, West Bloomfield, MI 48322, (888) 270-7583 phone, (248) 671-3874 fax, or made online at www.breakoutbrandstrategies.com.

Library of Congress Control Number: 2013903299

ISBN-13: 978-0-9890306-0-1

Limited of liability/disclaimer of warranty: While the publisher and the author have used their best efforts in preparing this book, they make no representations or warranties with respect to the accuracy or completeness of the contents of this book and specifically disclaim any implied warranties of merchantability or fitness for a particular purpose. No warranty may be created or extended by sales representatives or written sales materials. The advice and strategies contained herein may not be suitable for your situation. You should consult with a professional where appropriate. Neither the publisher nor author shall be liable for any loss of profit or any other commercial damages, including but not limited to special, incidental, consequential, or other damages.

For general information on our other products and services or for technical support, please contact our customer care department within the United States at RENEE WALKER & ASSOCIATES LLC, (888) 270-7583 phone.

Dedication

To Willie Elmo Walker, my grandfather and hero. He inspired us to reach for the stars and beyond; instilled in us an abiding faith, an unrelenting work ethic, and an uncompromising love of family and friends; and imparted a legacy of giving back and helping those who are in need.

To the Walker women—my mom, Shirley, my aunt and other mom, Flora, and my niece, Kelsey—who encourage, support, and inspire me every day.

To Kelvin and Garland, thank you for giving me the courage, tenacity, and unconditional love that lights my path forward. And thanks to my family who are both near and far.

To Renee, Deierdre, Judy, Michelle, Cathy, Dawn, Shawn, Rene, Brenda, Leslie, Nissi, and Alycia, thank you for being my sister-friends and for your unyielding love, support, motivation, and valued counsel.

Acknowledgments

I would like to express my sincere appreciation and gratitude to Jeff Orloff, Chas Withers, Gary Wells, Tyrone Jordan, and John Elsasser, who have inspired, encouraged, and supported me throughout my career. Your friendship and unyielding belief in my talents have enabled me to achieve my dream of authorship.

I also wish to express my deep appreciation to Nettie Seabrooks, a phenomenal woman whose grace, wisdom, and guidance have enabled me to expand my horizons and find my voice.

I'm forever grateful to Sue Ellen Eisenberg and Carissa Penna, extraordinary women who made it possible for me to pursue my entrepreneurial dream.

I wish to extend a heartfelt thank you to all who provided support, read, offered comments, allowed me to quote their remarks, and assisted with editing, proofreading, and design, with special recognition to Ryan Battishill for an amazing cover design, Jane Enos for exceptional editing, and Isha Cogburn for sharing her publishing knowledge with me.

And, finally, special thanks to Drexel Shingles and Lowell Kennedy, my glam squad—you're simply the best.

Contents

Renée T. Walker is president of RENEE WALKER & ASSOCIATES LLC, a WBENC-certified Women's Business Enterprise and a MMSDC-certified Minority Business Enterprise.

RENEE WALKER & ASSOCIATES LLC, a strategy and communications consultancy firm, has enjoyed rapid growth as Renée continues to build her successful consulting business that assists growth-stage start-ups to global organizations with harnessing their brand power, optimizing their competitive positioning, and driving their business growth.

Renée is an accomplished strategist, consultant, speaker, entrepreneur, and accredited public relations executive. She has nearly 30 years of strategic communications experience—including brand, public relations, crisis, reputation, public affairs, marketing, and higher education expertise—across the private, public, and nonprofit sectors. Renée offers and delivers a results-oriented and mission-driven focus to her clients.

Many distinguished organizations have invited Renée to share her executive communications perspectives and expertise as a presenter at national conferences and as a featured contributor in respected global-industry-related publications.

PART ONE
CHARTING YOUR COURSE

Introduction

"When it comes to the future, there are three kinds of people: those who let it happen, those who make it happen, and those who wonder what happened."
–John M. Richardson Jr.

Whether you're launching a new business or you're a seasoned business owner, you determine your destiny and guide your enterprise toward financial success and long-term viability. As an established small business entrepreneur or an aspiring business owner, you have the fortitude, commitment, and the requisite expertise and knowledge to manufacture products and deliver services. Perhaps, you even have achieved a large measure of success.

Entrepreneurship is a journey, not a destination. Are you on cruise control or looking to get into the fast lane? Are you looking to accelerate your business to the next level? Are you finding it difficult to distinguish your products, services, and company from your competition? Are you clueless about how to successfully market your offerings and generate solid customer leads?

Wherever you are on your entrepreneurial journey, *Brand Power for Small Business Entrepreneurs: Breakout Brand, Positioning, and Profit Strategies to Drive Revenue Growth* gives you the strategies, tools, and techniques successfully employed by highly credible, powerful, and profitable global companies to harness your brand power, create your competitive advantage, and propel your business to new heights without breaking your bank account.

It's time for you to employ these proven and savvy business strategies to maximize your return on investment by launching, reenergizing, or revving up your brand visibility and building a reputation for superior quality and service delivery.

As a passionate and veteran communications executive with nearly 30 years of experience directing brand, reputation, public relations, marketing, crisis, and public affairs programs across the private, public, and nonprofit sectors, I've written this book to share my advice, experience, and proven strategies with you—my fellow small business entrepreneurs.

With the successful launch of my strategy and communications consultancy firm, I've employed these strategies and techniques to establish a breakout brand for RENEE WALKER & ASSOCIATES LLC.

You too can achieve greater business and financial success and build a breakout brand that commands premium pricing and substantially differentiates you from your competitors. It's your time to make it happen. So turn the page and begin creating your road map for the next leg of your journey.

CHAPTER 2

A Hobby Business or an Entrepreneurial Enterprise?

"You can't do today's job with yesterday's methods and be in business tomorrow." –Unknown

Whether you've been in business for five days, five years, or decades or aspire to launch a business, a key decision is determining whether your business will be a hobby business or an entrepreneurial enterprise.

When planning your business, the most pressing decisions are usually deciding if you should indeed start a business, what products or services your business should offer, and the best legal structure for your start-up. While these are absolutely essential decisions, establishing your business endgame from the outset enables you to focus and optimize your knowledge, talents, resources, financial investment, and long-term opportunity for success.

If your business provides an opportunity for you to turn your passion, primarily, into supplemental or disposable income,

7

creating a sustainable, high-value brand isn't necessarily a priority to achieve your business and financial goals. That said, building a solid and consistent brand experience for your customers will only enhance your business opportunities and assist you in attracting loyal customers who become repeat customers.

On the other hand, if your small business enterprise is the principal source of your income, if you have employees, or if you endeavor to build your business for future generations or acquisition, creating a high-value, sustainable, and breakout brand is a business imperative.

The Small Business Administration defines a small business concern as one that is independently owned and operated, organized for profit, and not dominant in its field. Depending on the industry, size-standard eligibility is based on the average number of employees for the preceding twelve months or on sales volume averaged over a three-year period.

Your brand must differentiate your company, products, and services and effectively convey your value promise to create "top-of-mind" positioning, attract the coveted purchase-ready customers, and increase your profitability.

Yourdictionary.com defines a hobby business as the following: "An activity pursued without the expectation of making a profit. Losses experienced from a hobby are generally deductible only to the extent they can be used as an offset to hobby income. In other words, hobby losses cannot be deducted from other income. The IRS [Internal Revenue Service] assumes an activity is profit driven only if it results in a taxable profit in three of the last five years."

Of course, the Internal Revenue Service (IRS) has a definite opinion on this matter. So, if other factors don't motivate you, the business deductions and the financial and tax implications are good considerations when determining whether your business is a hobby or an enterprise.

There are rules for determining if an activity qualifies as a business and what limitations apply if the activity is not a business. According to the IRS website, "Incorrect deduction of hobby expenses account for a portion of the overstated adjustments, deductions, exemptions, and credits that add up to $30 billion per year in unpaid taxes."

To determine whether your business is a hobby or entrepreneurial enterprise, there are eight questions the IRS suggests you consider, including:

- Does the time and effort put into the activity indicate an intention to make a profit?

- Does the taxpayer depend on income from the activity?

- Does the taxpayer or do his/her advisers have the knowledge needed to carry on the activity as a successful business?

- Has the taxpayer made a profit from similar activities in the past?

- Has the taxpayer changed methods of operation to improve profitability?

So, here's the big question: Are you managing your company's brand as an entrepreneurial enterprise or a hobby business? If you aren't sure or haven't actively managed the brand for yourself or your business, there's still a tremendous opportunity to harness the power of your personal and company brand and create a competitive advantage.

Brands are big business as evidenced by the brand values of the top global brands released in October 2012 by Forbes.com on "The World's Most Powerful Brands" list. High-value brands create invaluable financial opportunity for these global companies and for the small business enterprises that harness their brand power.

While the top brands represent a wide array of industries, products, and services, they each convey a clear, concise, and well-known value proposition that elicits an emotional response or connection with their customers. As a result, individuals—whether they purchase these particular products or services—attached a value or worth to the brands based on their personal value judgments. They are aware of their existence and are familiar with them, even if their brand loyalty is placed elsewhere.

World's Most Powerful Brands, According to Forbes.com

Rank	Brand	Brand Value ($bil)	Consumer Perception Rank	Brand Revenue ($bil)	Industry
1	Apple	87.1	11	108.2	Technology
2	Microsoft	54.7	1	73.7	Technology
3	Coca-Cola	50.2	29	22.8	Beverages
4	IBM	48.5	20	106.9	Technology
5	Google	37.6	7	36.5	Technology
6	Intel	32.3	6	54	Technology
7	McDonald's	37.4	85	85.9	Restaurants
8	General Electric	33.7	49	124.7	Diversified
9	BMW	26.3	5	73.7	Automotive
10	Cisco	26.3	15	46.1	Technology
11	Oracle	25.9	50	37.1	Technology
12	Samsung	19.3	9	148.5	Technology
13	Disney	19	8	21.2	Leisure
14	Toyota	21.9	37	179.5	Automotive
15	Hewlett-Packard	18.3	13	127	Technology
16	Mercedes-Benz	21.8	54	88.2	Automotive
17	Louis Vuitton	24.5	93	8.8	Luxury
18	Gillette	16.8	14	8.3	Consumer Packaged Goods
19	Honda	20.9	62	96.2	Automotive
20	Nescafe	17.4	27	10.1	Beverages
21	AT&T	24.1	96	123.5	Telecom
22	Nokia	15.5	28	53	Technology
23	Budweiser	18.6	61	9.6	Alcohol
24	Wal-Mart	20.3	84	289.2	Retailing
25	L'Oréal	14.5	26	10.4	Consumer Packaged Goods
26	Nike	15.9	47	21.8	Apparel
27	Pepsi	16	48	13.5	Beverages
28	Amazon.Com	10.2	4	47	Technology
29	Visa	12.6	25	9.2	Financial Services
30	Siemens	13.6	40	100.7	Diversified

Source: http://www.forbes.com/powerful-brands/list/

Figure 1

For example, many households are loyal to certain brands due to the "perceived" value they place on the product or service. In Michigan, my home state and the home of the American automotive industry, generations of families are loyal to General Motors, Ford, or Chrysler vehicles because their family members earned their livings, purchased family homes, and provided for their children from building the vehicles.

For generations, these families have taken great pride in the manufacturing and purchasing of these vehicles. For these individuals, remaining brand loyalists is important to them and to their families. Other consumer products for which brand loyalty is usually high include laundry detergents, deodorants, sodas, and coffees—to name a few.

Brand loyalty—as defined by BusinessDirectory.com—is the extent of the faithfulness of consumers to a particular brand, expressed through their repeat purchases, irrespective of the marketing pressure generated by the competing brands.

Another key similarity among top brands is their position as category and industry leaders. This enables them to dominate their categories and markets.

Many entrepreneurs launch their companies and achieve some success, believing they can defer their brand development and management until their business is well-established, their financial house is in order, or their customer base is generating sufficient revenue.

These entrepreneurs are missing a key opportunity to attract purchase-ready customers, attain market share, and increase their profitability by building their brand value from the outset of their business enterprise. Eventually, as their market opportunities mature, economic conditions change, or their competitive landscape shifts, maintaining their market share and expanding into new customer segments will require repositioning and focused advancement of the company's brand.

If you're in the planning phase or in the process of launching your company, taking the required time to thoughtfully build your company's brand will provide immeasurable benefit to your market-entry opportunities and your long-term viability.

Seasoned business owners interested in expanding into new markets, increasing market share, attracting more purchase-ready customers, or growing their businesses will also benefit from taking stock of their brands to optimize market position and drive new business opportunities.

Employing the appropriate brand strategy for your business is a wise investment. While a successful brand strategy requires an investment, it doesn't require the outlay of millions of dollars. In fact, a well-planned and -targeted approach will provide considerable rewards for small businesses.

Often, entrepreneurs do considerable harm to their long-term success and their ability to drive revenue growth as they present an unprofessional and questionable presence to their potential customers.

According to an article published on February 13, 2011, on Forbes.com by Carol Kinsey Goman, "Researchers from

NYU found that we make eleven major decisions about one another in the first seven seconds of meeting." In today's ubercompetitive and crowded marketplace, the ability to stand out from your competitors, to effectively convey your value proposition, and to command the attention of high-value purchase-ready customers requires a strong, well-developed breakout brand strategy.

Beginning with your endgame in mind empowers you to envision your path forward. It enables you to lead your enterprise with strategic focus and purpose, resulting in your ability to leverage your resources and capitalize on your opportunities.

Whatever your endgame—an entrepreneurial enterprise or a hobby business—harnessing your brand power provides clarity, continuity, and conviction in establishing, reinventing, and repositioning your presence in the marketplace. A well-developed and -executed brand strategy is good business for global companies and for small entrepreneurial enterprises alike.

CHAPTER 3

Mapping Your Road to Success

"If we do not change our direction, we are likely to end up where we are headed." —Chinese proverb

With a clear direction to and a purposeful focus on your endgame, you can begin the strategic development process to build your brand, differentiate your products and services, and grow your business.

As your company's CEO, managing partner, owner, president, founder, or chief cook and bottle washer, you're one of its most valuable and visible assets. Knowing your strengths and gaps provides the information you need to leverage your personal brand and to expedite the positioning of your company for growth.

An honest and in-depth personal and professional assessment is an important first step to chart your road toward success. Perhaps you're thinking the following: I'm a super-busy entrepreneur who doesn't have enough hours in the day to complete my daily to-do list. With 18-hour workdays, sleepless nights, accounts payable, and the never-ending bombardment of e-mails, phone calls, sales calls, and meetings, I don't have the time or interest to complete another assessment. I need to make money!

But here are some critical considerations: Are your efforts, hard work, and resource investments delivering the results you desire? Are your investments paying off to your satisfaction? Is your company's brand adding value by differentiating your products and services from the competition? Are you effectively leveraging your competitive advantage by harnessing your brand power? Are you receiving a steady stream of purchase-ready customers, referrals, inquiries, and conversions?

If you answered "no" to any of these questions, assessing your strengths and strategically building a high-value brand to propel your company forward are essential to your short-term business and long-term financial successes.

There are a plethora of personality-, leadership-, and management-assessment tools available to measure any number of characteristics, deficiencies, and areas for improvement. Although knowing your improvement areas is necessary, identifying your strengths will enable you to effectively build your team and significantly enhance your opportunity for success.

In 2011, my dear friend and colleague Chas Withers, president and chief operating officer of Dix & Eaton, a

Cleveland-based communications consultancy firm, introduced me to StrengthFinders 2.0, a *Wall Street Journal*, *USA TODAY*, and *Businessweek* bestseller. It is one of the most recommended and preeminent leadership-assessment tools. Rather than identifying deficiencies, this tool enables you to discover your untapped talent and to coach others to develop their strengths.

This assessment tool provided great insight on my journey to entrepreneurship and served as an invaluable resource. It has enabled me to maximize my talents, make the most of my core competencies, and recalibrate my decision-making, problem-solving, and strategic-planning approaches.

If you already have completed StrengthFinders 2.0, it's time to dust off your Strengths Discovery and Action-Planning Guide and review your action plan. It provides sound information to jump-start your brand strategy. If you're unfamiliar with StrengthFinders 2.0, completing the assessment is highly recommended.

Another valuable self-inventory assessment exercise requires only a few hours to complete but can provide invaluable knowledge and perspective. As a result of your personal and professional experiences, you have continuously evolved and gained new insights, and over time, your priorities have likely shifted. Taking stock of your growth, priority shifts, and unrealized potential provides important insight and motivation to appropriately adjust your goals and objectives.

Understanding your personal brand is imperative as you lead your business forward. With this information in hand, you're well on your way to creating, rehabilitating, or leveraging a high-value breakout brand. When answering these assessment questions, give them careful thought.

- What are your core strengths?

- What are your core values?

- What are the five attributes that best define you?

- What are you most passionate about?

- What motivates you personally and professionally?

- Ask three to five trusted friends, colleagues, or family members to list your top three attributes. Do these attributes align with your self-assessment?

After completing the StrengthFinders 2.0 assessment and the self-inventory exercise, you should be able to clearly delineate your talents, capitalize on your strengths, and leverage your personal and professional brand.

With your personal assessment completed, you should evaluate your business strategy, market opportunities, and communication efforts. There are several key evaluation tools that will enable you to prepare a dashboard for assessing your efforts, identifying enhancement areas, and developing a focused and strategic action plan.

In his Visual Business Intelligence blog available at perceptualedge.com, Stephen Few defines a dashboard as "a visual display of the most important information needed to achieve one or more objectives; consolidated and arranged on a single screen so the information can be monitored at a glance."

When developing a dashboard for your organization, you should carefully define the key performance indicators (KPI) to track your progress toward achieving your established business and communication goals. Oftentimes, business owners focus on the KPIs solely related to their business goals, evaluating their communications in a silo or vacuum, if at all.

A more comprehensive and insightful approach is to incorporate your business and communication goals into a dashboard. This approach ensures that the communication strategies are aligned and directly contributing toward the attainment of the desired business outcomes.

Knowing the good, bad, and ugly of your business and communication efforts is necessary to transcend your current state and reach your desired market position.

When counseling and coaching my clients, I often use a variety of assessment tools to evaluate and benchmark their positioning and communication efforts, as well as their alignment to the business strategy—including branding, customer interactions, employee and stakeholder communications, marketing, and website. Using assessment tools provides an opportunity to gather critical insight about their communication efforts and facilitates a comprehensive review to identify strengths, weaknesses, missed and future opportunities, and ineffective communication programs.

There are many assessment tools that utilize an array of methodologies, inputs, and measures. The following assessment tools provide a wealth of information.

- **SWOT analysis.** This planning tool is used to evaluate the strengths, weaknesses, opportunities and threats (SWOT). It is most often used as part of business- and strategic-planning processes but also provides great insight when used in conjunction with organizational, departmental, and communication efforts.

- **Core competencies analysis.** This strategy tool is used to assess a company's ability to offer products or services, the relevancy of these competencies to the customer base and marketplace, the uniqueness of the company's products and services, the profitability the company generates (from its products or services), and the applicability of the products or services across multiple markets and customer bases.

- **Competitive analysis.** This strategic tool is used to assess your competitor's weaknesses and strengths, to forecast their reactions to specific market circumstances, and to improve your operations and offerings for increased market share or "top-of-mind" positioning.

- **Communications audit.** This assessment tool is used to evaluate the effectiveness and cohesiveness of a company's communications relative to its current and prospective customers, employees, stakeholders, constituencies, and public at large. It is a systematic assessment of the current communication methods and capacity, as well as the performance of essential communications practices.

- **Scenario analysis.** This strategy tool is used to forecast future situations and the varied factors and circumstances that could influence outcomes. It creates a framework to make informed and well-thought-out decisions and to test assumptions, providing a road map for capitalizing on opportunities and circumventing or responding to future challenges.

- **Value chain analysis.** This evaluation tool is used to identify opportunities that enhance the value of the products or services provided to your customers. It is very helpful when creating value-added opportunities that uniquely position and differentiate your company from your competition.

- **Website analysis.** There are several website-assessment tools that provide invaluable information regarding the effectiveness, usability, and performance of your website.

  Google Analytics provides comprehensive statistics regarding your website visitors, their behaviors, and engagement. This free tool also enables the tracking of visitor sources, specific communication, and marketing campaigns and actions.

  Hubspot's Marketing Grader evaluates your website and provides recommended enhancements to improve your marketing efforts. This tool also compares your website to your competitor sites.

These assessment tools can offer a comprehensive evaluation of a company's unique selling and value proposition. They substantially enhance your ability to communicate and engage with your customers and stakeholders, as well as improve your company's performance and positioning.

Following the completion of the assessment, create an actionable plan to guide your path forward and track your progress.

CHAPTER 4

Reflection, Research, and Reconnaissance

"Business, more than any other occupation, is a continual dealing with the future; it is a continual calculation, an instinctive exercise in foresight."
–Henry R. Luce

Reading, writing, and arithmetic. These three Rs represent the foundations of a basic skills-orientated program within our educational system. For business owners, these skills equate to customer targeting, conversions, and financial considerations.

However, as you build your brand and profit strategies, the original three Rs should take a hiatus as you focus on the foundational skills of reflection, research, and reconnaissance to successfully differentiate your company and its products and services and to take advantage of future business opportunities.

For the purposes of this book, reflection entails deciding if where your brand has been or where it's headed will likely yield the business outcomes and revenue results you desire. Do you have difficulty closing sales? Are you tilting at windmills in hopes of snaring that elusive megawatt deal and ignoring smaller, profitable, and potentially long-term customer relationships?

It is important to understand that your customer acquisition, sales, and revenue strategies are inextricably linked to your brand value. In Chapter 7, the tangible benefits of high-value brands and the impact on your business are discussed. Identifying your enhancement areas and developing an actionable and focused strategy enable you to envision new client acquisition, sales, and revenue approaches and to design new products and services offerings.

As a seasoned entrepreneur or an aspiring business owner, you know the necessity of reputable research data. It provides invaluable insight that can inform your business strategy and operational decision-making. Anticipating the industry trends, being customer focused, and providing value-added services are essential to gaining market share and industry visibility, which creates a significant competitive advantage in the marketplace.

In the areas of customer behavior and marketing personalization, data enables savvy business owners to focus on their customers' purchase-decision processes, to align their products and services to market needs, and to optimize marketing strategies across various customer segments.

When businesses fail to take advantage of customer behavior and marketing optimization opportunities by leveraging their high-value brand, lost opportunities due to their fragmented and often knee-jerk approaches result.

Typically, a one-size-fits-all marketing strategy is employed across all customer segments. However, this approach severely limits your ability to capitalize on the unique needs of your various customer segments and increases the likelihood that your marketing efforts will add to the deafening marketplace noise.

In today's highly competitive and cluttered marketplace, using data to gain deeper insight and micro-target customers to drive growth is imperative for your company's growth, long-term financial health, and sustainability. For small business enterprises, micro-targeting and brand amplification are no longer cost prohibitive. With the advent of content marketing, social media, and many cutting-edge and cost-efficient technologies, the playing field has been leveled for those entrepreneurs willing to invest in long-term success.

Although micro-targeting strategies, including data mining and predictive modeling to segment audiences and disseminate specific persuadable messaging to targeted groups, have been used in niche-consumer marketing for many, many years, they have received more visibility from successful use in President Obama's 2012 Presidential campaign. Micro-targeting also is easily applicable to business-to-business and business-to-consumer enterprises as well.

With insights acquired from reflection, research, and re-connaissance, entrepreneurs are equipped with the unique advantage of testing their business, product, and service models, optimizing the competitive landscape and micro-targeting strategies prior to implementation.

Observing the marketplace, anticipating customer trends, and identifying untapped market needs are your reconnais-sance goals. But, where do you begin?

Good starting points include subscribing to industry-related publications; using blog search engines, such as Technorati, Google Blog Search, and HootSuite, for social media con-versations that identify the most respected and influential industry and trade blogs; joining social media industry and customer groups; gathering demographic and socioeco-nomic data from the U.S. Census Bureau; and engaging in high-level targeted executive networking through private business clubs, trade associations, and civic organizations.

But most of all, listen to your customers, the industry ex-perts, and the marketplace to capture the information and data you need to succeed. Many business owners heavily rely on their intuition and beliefs related to their custom-ers' purchase motivators and pain points. They overestimate their ability to generate sales. Without the incorporation of adequate data, the assumptions that serve as the foundation for the sales and revenue generation often lead to unrealized potential and limited success.

Understanding your customers and their purchase-decision motivations and influencers—as well as discerning their future trends and pain points—affords you a competitive advantage and a unique market opportunity should you leverage them. The following questions should help you better identify and better understand these key drivers.

- What are the key value drivers that differentiate you among your peers and competitors?

- How do your key stakeholders, including customers, partners, employees, community members, and industry influencers, view your company?

- What are the buying behaviors of your customer segments?

- What are the key purchase-decision drivers for each customer segment?

- What outcomes are most critical for the long-term success of your business?

- What metrics or measures will be implemented to gauge progress over time?

Reflection, research, and reconnaissance are key components of your strategy formula to develop a value model that will guide your client acquisition, operations, and revenue-generation efforts.

While you should never completely discount your intuition, knowledge, and experience, having reliable, quantifiable, and objective data to inform your decisions is non-negotiable. Without adequate data, you're guessing and overlooking key information that will enable you to more effectively achieve your business objectives. As John Adams remarked, "Facts are stubborn things; and whatever may be our wishes, our inclinations, or the dictates of our passions, they cannot alter the state of facts and evidence."

When creating your reputation-value model, use reflection, research, and reconnaissance data for each of your customer segments. Asking and answering the following questions should help identify this data.

- What outcomes matter most to you as a business owner?

- What attributes or messages contribute most to your reputation, sales volume, and other key business or financial outcomes?

- What is the value of your reputation overall? What metrics should be used over time to measure progress or threats?

- What company attributes should be emphasized to your customers?

- What reputation attributes or messages about the company should you protect?

- When closing a sale, making a deal, or signing a client, what is the factoid, offering, or value statement that causes an "aha moment," winning you the business?

With your value model determined, acquiring comprehensive knowledge of your customers' decision processes and drivers—that is, the methods and motivations they use to select and purchase products and services—will enable you to strategically enhance your customer interactions, more effectively position your company and its offerings, engage your customer base, and understand how to build brand loyalty.

Generally, consumers and your customers, whether an individual, a company, or a corporation, employ a variety of behaviors and processes—including Internet searches, asking trusted individuals for referrals or recommendations, purchasing the most basic and cost-effective option to meet their unique needs, visiting physical stores to speak with informed sales representatives, or buying an item on sale—to purchase goods and services. In addition, they commonly use the following five-step decision process to arrive at their purchase decisions.

1. **Problem recognition.** When a need is perceived or created through marketing efforts, the consumer recognizes their desire for the product or service and begins to search for potential solutions.

2. **Search for alternative solutions.** The consumer will employ an array of information gathering methods, including personal referrals, Internet searches, and store visits, to identify the purchase options or explore high-value market-leading brands to clarify the various options that meet their unique needs and situations.

3. **Evaluation of alternatives.** With the options identified, the consumer assesses and compares these opportunities, including the relevant consequences, to make their purchase choice. Usually during this step, the consumer develops a value perception for each identified option.

4. **Purchase.** Prior to making the purchase, the consumer will consider the sale terms; return policy; previous experience with the brand, product, or service; and their shopping experience. The consumer selects and purchases the product or service that best satisfies their decision criteria, value assessment, and needs.

5. **Postpurchase reevaluation.** Following the purchase, the consumer will use the product or service

and evaluate its performance as compared to their established expectations and its ability to satisfy the intended need. This process will influence the consumer's repeat purchase, relationship development, or use of the applicable return policy, if appropriate.

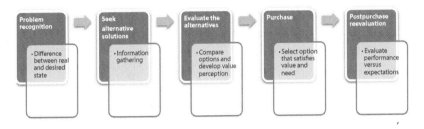

Figure 2

The five-step process put forth is a very basic introduction to the complex psychological theory of consumer behavior and the motivations or drivers that lead to purchase decisions. Marketing decisions, campaigns, and segmentation efforts are based on consumer behavior assumptions, including factors related to the following.

- External influences of demographics, culture, social status, family and reference groups, and marketing activities; the individual and society.

- Internal influences of perception, memory, personality, motivations, emotions, and attitudes of the purchaser.

Understanding your customers' purchase motivations, decision processes, and pricing considerations, as well as their value systems, enables you to forecast their likely responses and engagements with your company and its products and services. This is predictive information and should be utilized to develop your customer acquisition, marketing personalization, and revenue-generation strategies.

PART TWO
CREATING, REHABILITATING AND ENHANCING YOUR BRAND

CHAPTER 5

Brand Boot Camp

"Your premium brand had better be delivering something special, or it's not going to get the business." —Warren Buffett

There are millions of brand definitions, theories, webinars, seminars, print and electronic books, blogs, and websites offering various strategies, tactics, and best practices to create, manage, and advance your personal or company brand. By way of example, a Google search for "brand" yields about 126,000,000 results in 0.24 seconds.

For small business entrepreneurs or aspiring business owners, your brand is a critically important asset—one that requires your attention—and supports the successful growth or launch of your business. Yet, branding can be a very daunting and difficult undertaking. More often than not, branding is associated with a company's logo, look and feel, or color palette.

In a nutshell, brand, in its simplest and purist form, is what you say about yourself, your company, your value system, and most important, your promise to your customers. When a brand is successfully established, it has the credibility and power to substantively differentiate your business from that of your competitors.

As entrepreneur.com explains, "An effective brand strategy gives you a major edge in increasingly competitive markets. But what exactly does "branding" mean? Simply put, your brand is your promise to your customer. It tells them what they can expect from your products and services, and it differentiates your offering from your competitors. Your brand is derived from who you are, who you want to be and who people perceive you to be."

Your brand is communicated through your conduct, ethics, the quality of your services and products, customer experience, and communications. Without question, there are numerous myths and misconceptions regarding branding. So, let's dispel a few of the most prevalent.

Your brand is not a logo, tagline, color palette, or website. Your brand is a collection of perceptions from your employees, customers, and stakeholders. Brands are born from personal and customer experiences and reflect the reputation of your company. And in the case of sole proprietors, your brand reflects your personal and professional reputation.

Many believe you can build a quality brand by changing logos, creating new marketing materials, or emulating other successful companies. However, a successful high-value brand is built from the inside out over time. And, it is only as strong as your weakest brand touchpoint, including your personal conduct, company image, materials, website, product, service, and customer experience.

If your company's value proposition is excellent customer service but your customers experience a rude receptionist, encounter a dismissive customer service representative, or are unable to successfully resolve their concerns, your brand touchpoints do not reflect your value proposition.

Imagine you're a business owner and your brand promise is a high-value, high-touch customer experience. In other words, you've committed to providing your customers with an exceptional product or service and a customer-first experience. However, in reality, you and your staff don't promptly return customer telephone or e-mail messages and are nonresponsive or rude when customers need assistance or have difficulty with your product or service. Ultimately, your brand promise is not aligned with your customer experience.

Brand is what you say about yourself and your company.

Reputation is what others say about you and your company.

Effective brand management influences your reputation.

As previously mentioned, brand development and active management are prerequisites to your business and financial successes. Deferring your brand strategy development in favor of focusing on new client acquisition can create short-term gains but ultimately limits or impedes your long-term success and sustainable growth.

Another prevalent misconception among aspiring, newly established, and seasoned business owners is that they do not need external help when it comes to capitalizing on brand strategy. Perhaps they believe that hiring professional brand strategists or communication consultants is too expensive, that it is an unnecessary expense rather than a required investment for their business to succeed.

In fact, this is a very costly and often damaging belief since the development of your company's brand is viewed as an expense rather than a wise and savvy business investment. And what results is often a shotgun approach, yielding an unprofessional image and the inefficient expenditure of limited financial resources.

The impact of an unprofessional brand on your company's customer acquisition, revenue generation, and profitability can be staggering. Frequently, business owners do great harm to their business opportunities as potential customers devalue, downgrade, or dismiss their capabilities, products, or services as a result of interpreting the company's value promise, as conveyed by the unprofessional brand image. While you may provide outstanding products and phenomenal service to your customers, an unprofessional brand can mean you are frequently overlooked or excluded from business opportunities.

While there are many brand detractors and value inhibitors, the most frequent faux pas, mistakes, and missteps of small business entrepreneurs include the following.

1. Using AOL, Yahoo!, Gmail, sbcglobal.net, or other similar e-mail addresses for your business e-mail. These e-mail addresses are generally viewed as personal and free e-mail accounts accessible to everyone. Using these free and widely used e-mail accounts doesn't convey a successful, established, or competent business enterprise.

   This doesn't include the use of Gmail or other programs as an e-mail client or e-mail management system, similar to Microsoft Outlook or Apple Mail, where your e-mail address includes your website domain name.

2. Purchasing a website domain name and setting up an e-mail address without creating a professional website. Most potential customers or interested individuals will visit your website address—obtained from your domain e-mail address on your business card—to learn more about you, your company, your products, or your services prior to actually contacting you.

Your website is your single-most valuable communication vehicle and marketing tool. A nonexistent or unprofessional website often leads to missed opportunities as prospective customers will devalue your offerings and capabilities. If you don't have a website or your website turns your prospective customers off, they simply will not contact you.

3. Incorporating clip art as part of the company's brand and visual identity. Note the use of clip art should be avoided at all costs, unless your business enterprise offers products and services to children and families.

4. Creating "homemade" collateral, such as business cards, letterhead, envelopes, invoices, brochures, and flyers using desktop publishing software without the benefit of graphic design training or expertise. It is imperative your marketing brochures, stationery, business cards, and website are professional and coordinated and present a quality image.

5. Playing an inappropriate ringback tone—a song or message your callers hear prior to you answering their call or the call being placed into your voice mail—or ringtone when using your mobile phone for business.

6. Establishing unrealistic customer expectations by overcommitting, providing an inconsistent or a poor customer service experience, delivering inferior or defective products, or missing deadline commitments.

7. Employing self-serving networking practices to promote your company, products, or services. Time and again, business owners seek to hasten or bypass the mutually beneficial relationship-building process in favor of mass distribution of their business cards or marketing materials at networking events and other business gatherings.

8. Using a one-size-fits-all approach with regard to customer acquisition, marketing, and business strategy without a cohesive, actionable, and purposeful plan execution or no plan at all. Usually, the fly-by-the-seat-of-your-pants approach is extremely ineffective and significantly more costly.

These faux pas, mistakes, and missteps can result in significant damage to your brand—generating negative word of mouth, unrealized customer interaction, and a reputation for inconsistent or poor customer service—and can adversely affect your ability to positively stand out from your competition, to successfully promote your products and services, and to attract purchase-ready clients or customers.

Detrimental as they are, the good news is these brand detractors and value inhibitors are completely avoidable. With a clear sense of purpose, a keen understanding of your various customer segments, and the ability to articulate your value proposition, you can build a strong, breakout brand to achieve your business and financial goals.

Recognizing on average you have a mere seven seconds to make a first impression, you're placing unnecessary obstacles on your path to business success. While you can repair—with concerted effort and ample time—your brand with current and potential customers, you'll need to redirect your focus and resources to accomplish this turnaround. These resources would be more wisely invested in servicing your customers, generating qualified referrals, closing sales, and gaining market share.

Savvy business owners invest in their brands from the outset and position their business to create and seize customer opportunities. They continually advance and actively manage their brands to build equity and create a unique market position and competitive advantage.

Brands equal big business. Large organizations in the profit, nonprofit, and public sectors expend significant resources, including financial investment, to advance, direct, and protect their brands.

As illustrated in the Forbes.com chart in Chapter 2, global brands are valued assets and represent tens of billions of dollars in both tangible and intangible benefits to the company.

Companies with strong global brands tirelessly work to indoctrinate their value promise within their employee ranks, business operations, customer segments, suppliers, and the public at large. They actively cultivate, educate, and encourage their brand ambassadors to share and advance the company's brand.

Small business entrepreneurs and aspiring business owners would greatly benefit from the implementation of global brand strategies, appropriately adapting them to their unique business goals and market opportunities.

Successful brands are powerful. They provide impact in the marketplace, build trust, and evoke an emotional attachment within customers. Consider the following top global brands and their industry position.

- Apple's brand is one of the most powerful global brands and is valued at $87 billion according to the Forbes.com list. Apple's brand value has experienced exponential growth—resulting from the introduction of iTunes, iPod, iPhone, and iPad, as well as its brand clarity, consistency, and constancy.

  As the market leader known for revolutionizing the consumer technology sector and always pushing the envelope through innovation, Apple continues to provide exceptional customer focus, experience, and value. With its high-value brand, it commands premium pricing on its products and services.

- Cable News Network (CNN) is among the most trusted global media outlets, with its value proposition effectively communicated in the tagline "The

Worldwide Leader in News." CNN also extended their brand positioning to include "The Best Political Team on Television" in 2011.

- Tiffany & Co. is the epitome of high-quality and well-crafted jewelry. Established in 1837, Tiffany's commitment to its brand is formidable. Its packaging alone—including the registered Tiffany Blue Box® and its trademark ribbon—evokes overwhelming excitement when received as a gift due to the high-value proposition of the Tiffany brand.

Brands are valuable assets that contribute to the financial success of their companies. Building a clear, consistent, and constant brand for your company requires dedication, focus, and concerted effort.

In politics, perception is reality. For brands, perception is not simply reality—it is absolutely everything. Your brand lives in the minds of your consumers or customers. You must undertake an intensive, focused, and purposeful effort to ensure customer perceptions accurately reflect your intended value promise.

Why are brands important? Simple. A high-value breakout brand makes the selling process easier. It enables prospective and current customers to envision the value that your company, product, or service will provide to them prior to any sales presentation.

It also assists with attaining premium pricing as the value perceived by the customer has already been established. Customers who value your brand are more likely to expect a higher price for your product or service and are more willing to pay it. This enables you to increase your profit margins.

High-value brands also instill loyalty within your customer base as a result of your brand's credibility, authenticity, and value. This allows your company to withstand competitor and pricing wars or even an occasional product defect or service delivery problem.

As your competitors present their capabilities to potential clients, you're able to focus your efforts on resolving their problems and addressing their pain points as your high-value brand provides you a unique competitive advantage. Consider the worldwide recall of Toyota vehicles related to a problem with unintended acceleration. Although this recall resulted in billions of dollars in fines and received tremendous negative global media coverage, Toyota's brand was able to rebound and remains strong today.

Why did Toyota's brand recover so quickly? They spent many decades building equity in their brand. Toyota's brand can be summed up in one word—performance. As a result, when their vehicle performance failed them, Toyota moved to correct the problems, apologized to their customers, renewed their commitment to the performance and safety of their vehicles, and paid the government fines. And they were buoyed by the decades of exceptional customer service, the high performance, safety and reliability of their vehicles, and their commitment to building equity in the Toyota brand.

Building equity in your brand provides many financial benefits to your enterprise, including the following.

- **Increased awareness and market share.** With the marketplace offering various solutions and product options, a breakout brand with a high-value proposition and equity surpasses competitors.

- **Attraction of purchase-ready customers.** Imagine the competitive advantage you can enjoy with increased referrals and the attraction of purchase-ready customers based on awareness of your brand promise. From new to repeat customers, your brand is invaluable to your client and customer acquisition efforts.

- **Sustainable growth and long-term financial stability.** As an entrepreneurial enterprise, your brand can drive your revenue and business growth and contribute to your financial stability now and well into the future. Strong brands have staying power.

Many small business entrepreneurs never realize their brand potential. They're unable to effectively harness their brand power, optimize their competitive advantage, and drive their profitability. Instead, they opt for an ad hoc approach to their brand and marketing efforts, which results in unreliable and disparate customer experiences.

It's time for you to leave the stage and sit in the front row—to objectively and honestly review your business operations, products and service delivery, and customer service experience from the customer's perspective.

Here's your brand litmus test. Based on your knowledge of your company's operations, service delivery, product quality, and customer service experience, would you hire your company?

If you can honestly answer "yes," then list the attributes or reasons that influenced your response. For example, you may list that you continually go above and beyond to ensure customer satisfaction or that your quality-control process enables you to consistently manufacture products well below the industry-defect rate. Are these attributes potentially differentiating you from your competitors?

If you answered "no," then list the issues or challenges that support your response. These challenges must be addressed to ensure your customer experience is significantly improved and in alignment with your brand and value promise.

By investing the time and required financial resources to engage a professional team—including a brand or communications strategist, marketing researcher, graphic designer, website developer, and public relations specialist—savvy business owners will immeasurably enhance their brand and revenue-generation opportunities.

With this brand boot camp primer, you're equipped with the basic information to begin developing, enhancing, or amplifying your brand and positioning your company for even greater success.

You, Inc.

"If you don't drive your business, you will be driven out of business." –B.C. Forbes

Chapter 3 discusses the process of assessing your personal and professional strengths, talents, and weaknesses and evaluating your business and communication efforts. It is imperative that business owners understand how their personal brands can negatively influence or positively accelerate the attainment of their business goals.

Your personal brand and reputation can be the foundation of your success or an impediment to it. Understanding that you are the message as it relates to your business, your customers, and your products or services is of paramount importance.

Your reputation—what others say about you—is a powerful and impactful reality. It is up to you to ensure that your reputation is aligned with who you are and your core values and that it consistently articulates and leverages your unique value proposition.

Many small business owners fail to connect the dots between their personal and professional brands and their company's brand. And in so doing, these business owners are missing a key component to their overall business strategy— creating their competitive advantage through clear, concise, and purposeful communication of their brand promise.

Recognizing the value of your personal and professional reputation—the generally held perception about you, your credibility, and your capability—enables you to determine if you should amplify, rehabilitate, or enhance your brand. Remember, you can most effectively influence your reputation through the building, managing, and advancing of your brand.

For example, if you're well-known and highly regarded in your industry as a competent, capable, and respected professional, your ability to attract, engage, and secure customers for your enterprise will be made easier. Your valuable reputation will precede you in the marketplace, attracting interested and qualified customer leads. You will rise above the marketplace clutter with an opportunity to substantively differentiate yourself from your competitors.

Now, if you are unknown in your industry and market sector, have a reputation for poor customer service, or present an unprofessional or undiscerning image, your ability to attract customers will be greatly hindered. You will need to redirect significant resources to rehabilitate your reputation. While this is very doable, it is no easy task and requires ample time and continual near-perfect execution.

At this point, you might be thinking that you can simply fake it until you make it with regard to your brand and reputation and that the one-size-fits-all marketing and communication approach you're using will deliver the desired business results.

In order to amplify, rehabilitate, or enhance your brand, you must own up to your reputational deficiencies and embrace them as character-building opportunities. A poor or undefined reputation does not have to be fatal, but correcting it must become your top priority. It must be immediately and successfully addressed.

The rules of engagement when you're amplifying, rehabilitating, or enhancing your reputation through proactive and focused brand management are as follows:

- **Be authentic.** Your brand must become a true reflection of your value system, beliefs, and unique value proposition. You can't borrow from and emulate other people or your competitors. For your brand to have value, it must be a clear and true expression of your value promise and must be conveyed throughout all of your brand touchpoints.

- **Be diligent.** A focused and dedicated approach to your brand is a must. Consistently advance and protect your brand value and attributes and ensure your customer experience is above reproach. If negative word of mouth has occurred, you must address it immediately.

  This doesn't mean you should confront the individuals or dissatisfied customers. But, you should own up to any perceived or accurate deficiencies in your previous service delivery, customer interactions and experiences, or product deficiencies and take the appropriate actions to correct them.

- **Be consistent.** With the previous deficiencies addressed both operationally and within your customer base and industry, you must consistently provide superior products and service delivery. No exceptions are permitted.

  You also must exceed all customer expectations and offer value-added service to assist your customers with addressing their unique needs and with solving their problems. You must pay close attention to all details in your product and service delivery, with careful thoughtfulness paid to your customer interactions.

- **Be relevant.** If you have been in business for sometime or if you're launching your business, you must actively listen to your customers and the marketplace to ensure your services and products are timely and remain relevant. For those business owners who continuously seek to improve their services and products, your goal is to remain ahead of the curve.

If you continue to do what you have always done or if you're entering the marketplace providing identical products and services as your competitors (even when you're providing exemplary service and solid products), you will become out of step with the market and will not be noticed at all.

- **Be purposeful.** While admirable, having the best intentions is simply not good business. You must be purposeful in your interactions with your current and prospective customers. And equally as critical, you must ensure that your brand and reputation are accurate reflections of your value promise.

There are many personal and company brand touch-points that must be aligned to build trust, credibility, and value for your company, products, and services. Every person or company has a brand image and reputation—either intentionally or unintentionally. Individuals and companies that actively and purposefully direct, advance, and protect their brand value are intentional in their management efforts. Conversely, those who don't engage in their brand management have a significant disadvantage.

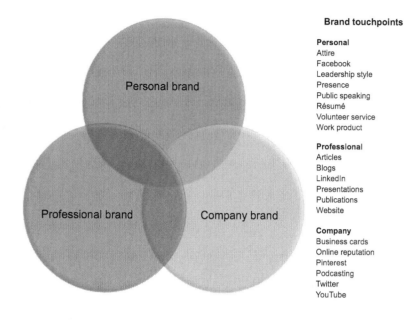

Figure 3

As depicted in Figure 3, your personal leadership style, past speaking engagements, integrity, and attire present an image and value proposition that transfers to your company as its chief executive officer. Your customers and prospective customers will continually evaluate and assess your competence, value, and capabilities to meet their needs through the direct contact and experience with your personal and company images or touchpoints.

In today's highly competitive marketplace, presenting a well-articulated image in a cohesive manner will aid in building confidence and trust with your current and prospective customers. Leveraging your personal brand can yield immeasurable benefits—including enhanced differentiation from your competitors, increased sales, and credibility among your customer base—to your company's business and financial success.

Building a Breakout Brand

> *"The leader who exercises power with honor will work from the inside out, starting with himself."*
> *–Blaine Lee*

Let's start with a brief recap. Your company's brand lives in the minds of your employees, customers, and many stakeholders. It is the total sum of their direct and indirect encounters with your company, its products and services, and its promise to them.

Your brand is the promise that your company makes on a daily basis and is the essence of what your company believes it is providing in value.

Whatever your business, products, or services—from manufacturing widgets to providing professional services—your brand matters and requires your thoughtful attention.

Successful brands convey a simple, easy-to-understand concept that encompasses both current and aspirational goals.

Delivering your brand promise via consistent, purposeful, and authentic interactions with your customers, employees, and stakeholders will serve as the foundation for your business success.

A breakout brand is customer centered, forward focused, and imaginative and builds credibility, visibility, and a reputation for quality that contributes to the organization's financial viability.

Building a strong, breakout, and profitable brand takes time and a concerted effort from you, your employees, and your key stakeholders. There are six steps to building a breakout brand that adds value to your business and enables you to leverage your competitive advantage.

1. **Inventory your brand equity.** It's time to get real about your current brand identity, its current equity, or its lack of identity. If, currently, your brand is being devalued or inhibited, you must move swiftly and purposefully to address weaknesses and impediments. If you previously deferred the purposeful management of your brand, it's time for you to get in motion.

2. **Define your desired brand identity, its attributes, core values, and value promise.** Using your company and personal brand assessments, create a go-forward actionable strategy to establish credibility

and believability by remaining committed to your core values.

3. **Align your brand touchpoints.** Prior to launching your updated brand publicly, you must take adequate time to align your brand touchpoints internally. This alignment includes:

   a. Engaging a team of professionals—which might include business coaches, strategists, and marketing and public relations experts—to assist you with developing and executing your alignment efforts.

   b. Training your employees to ensure they are performing their duties in ways that coincide with your brand promise. They need to be able to articulate and incorporate the value promise throughout your business operations.

   c. Updating your company communication channels—including customer contacts and correspondence, website, marketing brochures, letterhead, business cards, social media platforms, and advertising—to present a concise, consistent, and cohesive articulation of your value promise.

4. **Build credibility and trust and increase your visibility.** Enhance your reputation with third-party accolades and testimonials and attain

industry-respected and -valued certifications and awards. All awards are not created equally, as many are not recognized or valued across the industry establishment.

5. **Launch your new brand.** With your employees, stakeholders, and customers on board, the implementation of a well-defined, strategic brand launch will enable your company to begin the market repositioning process. It is critical that you actively manage, leverage, and protect your new brand positioning and build equity in the marketplace and within the communities you serve. Remain consistently true to your brand, and immediately address any obstacles or issues.

6. **Measure and realign your brand.** Your brand should be dynamic and continuously evolving to remain relevant to your current and future customers. Align your measurements to your business goals. Tracking your results, adjusting your approach, as appropriate, and driving improvements based on your data are the keys to your success.

Building a breakout brand

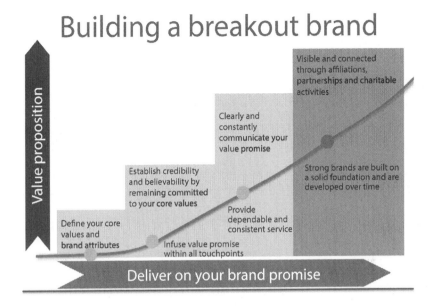

Figure 4

There are several building blocks to create a profitable breakout brand, including an actionable and well-defined strategy, a clear voice, a consistent visual identity, proactive management, and a reliable customer experience as illustrated in Figure 4.

Another essential element to building a breakout brand is cultivating highly motivated and passionate brand ambassadors. These individuals are loyal to your brand and actively or passively promote it. Brand ambassadors are not limited to you, your marketing employees, other employees, or your leadership team. Breakout brands foster ambassador relationships with their customers, vendors, community members, and the public at large. In the retail sector, consider the amount of logoed designer apparel, bags, luggage, and shoes or the retail stores that provide logoed bags for customer purchases.

Smartphone and tablet manufacturers like Apple and Google respectively program the default e-mail signature as "Sent from my iPhone" or "Sent from my Android." This tactic is part of their brand-ambassador strategies. Brand ambassadors also place an identifiable "face" on your company, customers, products, and services.

The formula to build a breakout brand consists of three elements: 1) creating a solid voice, visual identity, and value-added enhancements that support and convey your brand promise; 2) aligning your brand touchpoints, including your website, marketing materials, internal and external communications, business strategies, operations, and resources; and, 3) establishing credibility and visibility in the marketplace to influence your reputation. Figure 5 illustrates the formula to build a breakout brand.

Companies with breakout brands align their brand and business strategies. From syncing these strategies, they harness their brand power, optimize their competitive advantage, and drive their business success. They also are able to command premium pricing and experience higher customer-satisfaction rankings, increased customer and brand loyalty, repeat business, and a greater return on their investment.

Breakout brand formula

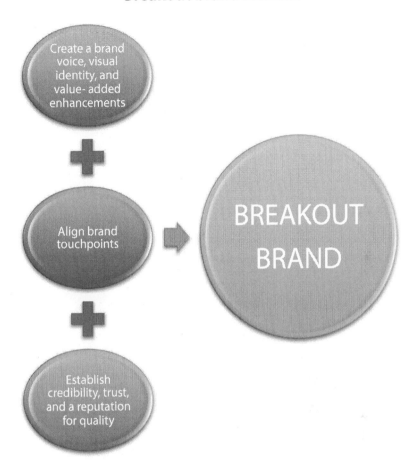

Figure 5

CHAPTER 8

Creating a Winning Team

> *"In the end, all business operations can be reduced to three words: people, product, and profits. Unless you've got a good team, you can't do much with the other two." –Lee Iacocca*

Whether you build an internal employee-based team, engage external consultants and freelancers, or use a hybrid approach to acquire the talent you need, hiring the right team or group of employees requires considerable forethought and planning.

As you begin your talent-acquisition process, will you work with professionals, including employees, consultants, or freelancers, or take a do-it-yourself approach? At first blush, the do-it-yourself approach probably appears the easiest, fastest, and cheapest method. In actuality, however, this approach often is more costly due to the loss economies of scale, the need to redo deliverables as a result of errors and omissions, a steep learning curve, missed business opportunities, and the increased investment of your time and effort. It's counterintuitive that working with experienced consultants and freelancers or hiring top talent is likely the most cost-efficient approach.

Experienced consultants, freelancers, and highly skilled employees enable business owners and entrepreneurs to focus on their core competencies, business operations, and customer-acquisition efforts. These professionals also bring their networks of designers, writers, editors, printers, and the like to the team and can employ cost-effective methods, saving you valuable time and money while increasing your return on investment.

If you use a haphazard approach or forego the appropriate due diligence, you'll hire the wrong consultants or employees, resulting in wasted time and resources, incomplete or incorrect deliverables, unattained goals, and missed opportunities—all at a premium cost.

Likewise, if you hire the right employees or consultants to provide their expertise but you're unclear about your desired outcomes, the company culture does not support the go-forward plan, or you're not fully committed to building a strong, profitable, or breakout brand, your efforts will be severely hindered and additional time and financial investment will be required to address these challenges.

Hiring the best employees, consultants, or freelancers exponentially enhances your ability to accomplish the desired business and brand outcomes. The personal, professional, and company assessments discussed in earlier chapters will be invaluable when it comes to attracting, hiring, engaging, and retaining the talent you need to succeed.

As you review your assessment and evaluation results, it is critically important that you determine the skills, expertise, collaboration, knowledge, and other attributes that are required to build or enhance your team. Another consideration is determining your need for a strategist or a tactician to direct the work from concept through execution.

Strategists are conceptual thinkers who are able to use data and insight to undertake a long-range view, to align goals, and to plan resources and a course of action that achieve the desired goals and objectives.

Strategists often use a variety of modeling and scenario methodologies to forecast and address potential unforeseen obstacles, challenges, and opportunities that could affect the achievement of the desired outcomes. They also employ a series of metrics or measurements that evaluate and modify the plan to ensure alignment toward the desired goals.

Conversely, a tactician provides planned support of programs or campaigns and deals with the implementation or execution of actions to resolve or address particular problems or opportunities. Frequently, tacticians are focused on the present situation with little to no consideration for future challenges, opportunities, or unintended consequences.

So, how can you determine if you need a strategist, a tactician, or both? You must determine if you need assistance with a broad-view program or simply the implementation of a specific campaign. For example, both binoculars and microscopes magnify objects. Generally, you would choose binoculars (strategists) to obtain a three-dimensional view and to bring far away objects closer. Microscopes (tacticians), on the other hand, enable you to view objects unseen by the unaided eye. Each offers unique opportunities and benefits just as strategists and tacticians do.

Hiring a highly qualified and talented consultant or employee doesn't have to be a daunting and unmanageable task. The following strategies will assist you in your search.

- **Define your needs.** Finding the right consultant requires you to effectively articulate your needs, expectations, and goals, taking into consideration your collaborative and leadership style, company culture, and whether you need the expertise of a strategist or tactician.

- **Ask for referrals.** Engaging your network of trusted confidantes, share your needs and request recommendations for consultants or professionals they have successfully engaged.

- **Conduct interviews and check references.** As with hiring employees, the consultant or freelancer will have access to your company's proprietary and most sensitive information. You should exercise all due caution when interviewing the consultants and their references. A bad hire could significantly diminish or hinder your progress.

Develop a questionnaire with mostly open-ended questions, and jot down the key responses you believe are important prior to the conversation. If this process is overwhelming, ask your network or trade association to identify a few senior-level communication executives that you could consult in preparation for this process.

- **Distribute a request for proposal (RFP).** The RFP process doesn't need to be very time consuming. Using the needs you defined for the engagement, prepare a brief RFP with the key information and require a breakdown of the response components and their associated costs. This approach will enable you to compare the proposals and comprehend the different recommended approaches and deliverables.

- **Break the desired outcomes into phases.** There are advantages to awarding the work in one contract, namely pricing advantages. But, by phasing the work, you will have the opportunity to evaluate the consultant's approach and contribution to your goals prior to committing a significant financial investment.

Both strategists and tacticians offer skills, expertise, and knowledge to their companies and clients. Indeed, strategists and tacticians commonly work together on projects of all sizes.

If you determine the best approach for your situation is the do-it-yourself one, follow the aforementioned strategies when engaging the resources and vendors you'll use. There also are a number of crowdsourcing websites. Mashable.com defines crowdsourcing as "distributed problem solving" and states that from "distributing tasks to a large group of people, you are able to mine collective intelligence, assess quality, and process work in parallel."

There are numerous crowdsourcing websites that provide branding, visual identity, editorial, website development, video production, and graphic design services. Although a small sampling of sites follows, this is neither an endorsement nor recommendation for usage.

- Fiverr.com

- Elance.com

- Crowdspring.com

- Odesk.com

There are many ways to create and configure your team. With the advent of crowdsourcing, the conventional team—everyone working as an employee with traditional business hours—is now obsolete. Engaging consultants and freelancers or employing crowdsourcing provides an affordable, flexible, and customizable talent pool.

Whatever your team configuration, a word of caution is in order. Always make sure you own the rights to the work produced for your company. This is particularly important when working with consultants, freelancers, or crowdsourcing websites.

PART THREE
HARNESSING YOUR BRAND POWER

CHAPTER 9

Your Brand Strategy in Action

> *"Profit in business comes from repeat customers, customers that boast about your project or service, and that bring friends with them."*
> *—W. Edwards Deming*

As you prepare your brand strategy, an important first step is assessing your current brand value or equity, your company's readiness to actively support the strategy, and your ability to execute the strategy.

Many small business entrepreneurs struggle to succinctly articulate their product and service offerings and, even more significant, their value proposition. So, how effectively can you guide your business to financial success? And, how will your prospective customers identify you as a viable or preferred option if you're unable to communicate your ability to meet their needs?

The following assessment statements will evaluate your ability to create, articulate, manage, promote, and advance your company's brand. When considering these, think about if they occur never, rarely, sometimes, often, or always.

1. You and your employees understand how your customers feel about your products and services based on qualitative or quantitative data.

2. You actively study what is most important to your current and prospective customers, using face-to-face interviews, survey questionnaires, or other formal research methods.

3. Your company's culture, organizational structure, and operations are aligned with your brand-value promise.

4. When hiring and on-boarding employees, your brand promise and the role it plays in enhancing your market position is provided to new employees.

5. You and your employees clearly articulate your unique selling proposition and key differentiators.

6. You and your employees understand how to deliver your brand promise and actively perform your responsibilities in this manner.

7. Your performance evaluation process includes an assessment of your employee's contribution to building and enhancing your brand.

8. Your business operations, including product production, finance and human resources, service delivery, and marketing and communications functions, are aligned to your brand promise.

9. You engage a brand or communication strategist as a strategic partner and actively involve him or her in the organizational and communications-planning and -evaluation processes.

10. You regularly communicate your brand promise to your employees and provide them with the required information and tools to successfully support and advance the brand.

11. You continually look for innovative and effective ways both internally and externally to build brand value, recognizing that strengthening and protecting the company's brand is a fundamental driver for long-term financial success.

12. Your brand strategies are proactive and include your partners and key suppliers and are not determined by your competitors' strategies.

If you responded never or rarely to the majority of the aforementioned statements, you have considerable internal work to perform prior to executing your brand strategy.

There are several components to creating your brand strategy and effectively articulating your brand promise. These include your brand's voice, visual identity, and value-added enhancements.

Your brand voice represents your company's personality and shapes your brand identity. Your voice is unique to your company, products, and services. It should be difficult to replicate, consistently reflected in every communication medium, and represented in a clear, concise, and credible articulation of your brand promise.

The following brands have created a consistent voice that spans beyond their current or future advertising or marketing efforts; their voices reflect the essence of their core brand promise and are consistently communicated through their visual identities, print materials, digital properties, graphics, and advertising.

Company	Brand voice
Apple	Innovation
FedEx	Efficiency
Walmart	Value
Weight Watchers	Empowerment

According to a December 14, 2011, Forbes.com blog post, entitled The Real Story Behind Apple's 'Think Different' Campaign, by Rob Siltanen, Apple launched its campaign in 1997 that began with these words:

"Here's to the crazy ones. The misfits. The rebels. The troublemakers. The round pegs in the square holes. The ones who see things differently. They're not fond of rules. And they have no respect for the status quo. You can quote them, disagree with them, glorify, or vilify them. About the only thing you can't do is ignore them. Because they change things. They push the human race forward. And while some may see them as the crazy ones, we see genius. Because the people who are crazy enough to think they can change the world, are the ones who do."

Clearly, Apple is adept at conveying their brand voice, personality, and promise.

Working with a brand strategist, you will develop your brand voice as the foundation of your overall brand strategy. This process will inculcate who you are, what your company stands for, and where you're headed. Creating your unique brand voice also requires you to identify the most effective communication strategies, channels, and operating structure and to align these to your brand personality.

This ensures your communication style conveys and supports your brand promise. Finally, transfer this knowledge to your employees and stakeholders and provide them with the required training and tools to effectively infuse your brand voice into all aspects of their performance, decision-making, and communications.

Using your brand voice and personality, your attention should now turn to creating your visual identity. Most often, business owners and entrepreneurs focus on their logo and color palette without the benefit of developing their unique brand voice. This approach is very costly and usually results in the creation of multiple business card designs, inconsistent visual representation, and a significant distraction to building brand equity.

When selecting a color palette for your visual brand identity, it is highly advisable that you engage a graphic designer who understands the use of colors, their applicability across digital, print and broadcast mediums, and the emotions and responses they evoke. For example, red is bold and communicates caution or, in the case of traffic signals, to stop. Blue is generally perceived as a cool and calming color. It is popular with airlines, hospitals, and corporations. Purple is most often associated with nobility or royalty. It evokes a sense of luxury and power. Choosing the colors that best convey your brand and that are usable across multiple platforms requires careful thought and professional expertise.

While there are a number of companies that provide graphic design services targeted toward small business owners, such as FedEx Office, Staples Copy and Print, Vista Print and Overnight Prints, caution should be the order of the day.

Careful thought should be given to using these services without the engagement of a consultant or professional graphic designer; this ensures your voice is effectively communicated through your visual identity.

If you're of the opinion that having a business card, website, or marketing materials is better than not having them, you're likely to squander your opportunity to make a lasting and positive first impression. You can personally engage with potential customers, as your visual identity is being developed or rehabilitated.

Simply ask for the contact's business card. Or, obtain an application for your tablet that enables you to capture their contact information and subscribe to future communications and contacts. You can also capture their business card with your phone's camera or with an application.

When engaging a graphic designer or other creative talent, it is important to clearly articulate your vision, brand voice and personality, and desired brand image. Generally, this is accomplished by preparing a creative brief—a short document that provides the graphic designer, videographer, copywriter, or other creative talent with a succinct overview of the most significant issues to consider in the development of your visual identity.

When preparing your creative brief, it is imperative to provide the following information.

- Provide an overview of the project and the desired deliverables (e.g., logo, stationery, note and business cards, brochure, color palette, etc.).

- Describe your brand promise, voice, and personality, as well as your key differentiators.

- Provide your value-added enhancements.

- List your customer segments and industries you serve.

- Provide the three most important messages you want to convey.

- Describe the tone, imagery, or emotional pull you want to evoke or the impression you want to convey.

The overarching purpose of the creative brief is to define your project and desired outcomes to ensure everyone working on the project has a clear and comprehensive understanding of your vision, strategy, and project goals. A well-written and concise creative brief will enable the project to proceed efficiently and produce the best results.

With your visual identity in development, creating your launch plan to introduce or reintroduce your company and its brand requires considerable thought and planning. Your goals should be to leverage your new or improved brand to cultivate your brand ambassadors, engage current and former customers, enhance your relationship with your employees, and build awareness with prospective customers.

Your brand launch should be purposeful and well-executed and successfully convey your brand promise. It should elevate your company, products, and services. You will need to develop an internal rollout for your employees, customers, and other key partners and stakeholders. You also will want to generate considerable buzz with your external audiences and industry.

Your brand launch should bring your brand to life and begin to establish or enhance your credibility and reputation for quality. Appropriately planning your launch is a necessity.

- **Develop your brand launch strategies.** How will you engage your employees, customers, influencers, and other key stakeholders and promote your new brand? How will you generate "buzz" and build awareness of your brand?

- **Create an action plan and timeline.** These planning tools are extremely helpful to a successful launch. It is paramount that you prioritize and strategize the manner in which your audiences and stakeholders will become aware of your new brand to ensure you're building support and momentum.

  For example, one of the biggest missed opportunities can occur when external audiences, such as your customers and suppliers, learn of your new brand prior to engaging and inculcating it within your employee groups and internal operations. Generally, you want to engage and empower your employees and ensure your operations are aligned with the brand promise.

It also is prudent to build in ample production and purchasing time for any advertising or printing requirements, including invitations, marketing materials, website launch, etc.

- **Establish your budget.** Remember this is an investment in the long-term success and financial health of your company. While an extravagant and pricey display might be nice, it is not necessary and could be harmful to your customer relationships and future prospects. Your budget should support your brand promise. Period.

If you expend or give the impression that you are spending considerable resources when your brand voice, personality, and promise support high quality at a reasonable price point, you're sending the wrong message and are in direct conflict with your brand. Let's suppose you need to increase your pricing in six months. Your customers could remember your over-the-top brand launch and resent the increase, opting to purchase from your competitors.

Your brand launch is not the time for "champagne wishes and caviar dreams"—a phrase made famous by Robin Leach, host of *Lifestyles of the Rich and Famous*—unless, of course, your brand is aligned with this very vivid and expensive image. For instance, a no-expense-spared launch may be appropriate for high-end luxury brands for which customers not only expect it but also require it.

- **Hire professionals to optimize your resources.** If you don't have employees who are able to professionally strategize, manage, and execute your launch, hire consultants to perform the work or advise you and your team. In the long run, you'll save time, resources, and money.

- **Measure your results.** As with all great programs or plans, determine what success will look like, track your progress, and measure your results.

- **Remember to say "thank you" and mean it.** In today's fast-paced and instant-gratification world, the art of saying "thank you" has been greatly diminished. However, conveying heartfelt gratitude or expressing your sincere appreciation to your employees, customers, brand ambassadors, and supporters is essential.

A well-executed and successful brand launch will go a long way toward rehabilitating your brand, elevating your company, and attracting your future business opportunities. Proceed wisely and thoughtfully because your future could depend on it.

CHAPTER 10

Game Changers and Business Accelerators

"The entrepreneur always searches for change, responds to it, and exploits it as an opportunity."
–Peter Drucker

Building a breakout brand requires more than relationships, a logo, know-how, or an actionable strategy. It requires you to align your business-operation, brand, customer-acquisition, and revenue-generation strategies. This is the foundation for success employed by global billion dollar companies.

Your business success requires a comprehensive assessment, sound business strategies, and precise execution. From knowing their strengths to determining their capacity for growth, savvy business owners and entrepreneurs strategize their business opportunities, formalize their plan, and realize their financial goals through focused execution to ensure a superior product and service delivery.

Understanding how to evaluate your capacity, identify your customer strike zone, and create a strategic plan is a game changer that will support your continued growth, create a competitive advantage, and leverage your resources for a greater return on your investment.

In the October 10, 2012, Forbes.com article, "6 Steps for Creating a Game Changer," Mike Myatt had this to say about game changers: "Leaders who pursue game changers have no patience for the status quo—they focus their efforts on shattering the status quo. Game changers refuse to allow their organizations to adopt conventional orthodoxy and bureaucracy—they challenge norms, break conventions, and they encourage diversity of thought. The message here is a simple one—don't copy, create. Where you can't create, improve on, and innovate around best practices to find next practices."

What are your customer-acquisition and revenue-generation strategies? Your customer-acquisition strategies are the processes you undertake to acquire new customers—from generating customer leads through conversion activities— and to accelerate your business growth. These strategies employ consumer-behavior and purchase-decision drivers to persuade, influence, and engage your prospects.

Oftentimes, customer-acquisition strategies for small business enterprises are as effective as throwing spaghetti on the wall to see what sticks. If you attend business functions, networking events, or approach potential customers without a definitive strategy, you're squandering a great opportunity to seize the moment.

Finding your strike zone and target-rich environments requires research, forethought, and planning. Many times, small business owners tell me their plan is to distribute their business cards and marketing materials to every person they meet. Unfortunately, this less than strategic approach is reinforced by printing company advertisements and by the proliferation of business networking events.

Dictionary.com defines networking as "a supportive system of sharing information and services among individuals and groups having a common interest: Working mothers in the community use networking to help themselves manage successfully." The key to successful networking is not the quantity of the business cards you receive, distribute, or exchange but rather the quality of the mutually beneficial introductions you make and the relationships you can establish.

When attending business functions or networking events, identify a select few individuals with whom you can share mutually beneficial information. Or, single out those whom you think your products and services can most help. You should not expect to collect or distribute 50 or more cards at these functions, unless you're in a target-rich environment and the interactions are within your strike zone.

If you're not currently utilizing a strategic approach to your customer-acquisition efforts or you're pursuing the megawatt deal without the benefit of a cohesive and achievable strategy, you are basically tilting at windmills. These approaches are fine if you can afford them.

For those who are actively working to build a business and achieve financial health and long-term sustainability, tilting at windmills simply is not an option. You must consider the "opportunity cost"—as defined by businessdirectory.com as a benefit, profit, or value of something that must be given up to acquire or achieve something else—of your customer-acquisition efforts. For example, let's say you have the opportunity to bid on two contracts that will limit available capacity during a specific time period. As a result, you forego other business opportunities that may be larger and more profitable. Your opportunity cost, then, is the loss of your missed opportunities that result from your decision to pursue the bid jobs that will absorb your available capacity.

Have you ever considered your time, resource, and financial investment related to your customer-acquisition efforts (e.g., trade show participation, conferences, travel expenses, mileage and gas receipts, event fees, meals and entertainment—to list a few)? These expenditures can be significant. Have you calculated your return on investment or your acquisition cost per customer or activity?

Generally, the return on investment discussion is focused on the marketing and communication expenditures. It is important that you include your customer-acquisition efforts as well.

As previously discussed, a one-size-fits-all approach to your marketing and communication efforts isn't the most effective or cost-efficient way to persuade and attract customers. Employing the strategies of successful brands and market leaders is very feasible and can create a breakout brand for your small business enterprise.

First, begin with the company's most valuable and achievable three to five business goals. For each goal, determine how communications can most effectively support the goal achievement.

Next, while remembering that a one-size-fits-all approach is counterproductive, determine the customer segments that you want to reach with the communications, communication channels, and platforms that will most efficiently and successfully deliver your messages with the highest impact among your intended audience.

For each customer segment, develop strategies, goals, objectives, tactics, and activities that optimize the identified communication channels. Then, determine the most persuasive messaging points for distribution through the specified channels.

Using your previous analyses, dashboard, and key-performance indicators, benchmark your current status to quantify any gaps that exists. This information enables you to measure your progress and results and assists with prioritizing your strategies, resources, and investments.

Brand and business alignment process

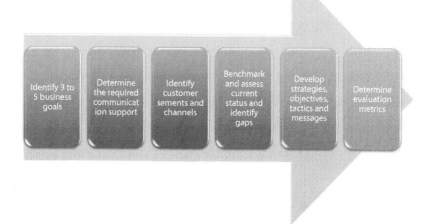

Figure 6

There are many cost-effective and free communication tools available to support your brand strategy and to propel your reputation development. Generally, these are organized within the buckets of earned, owned, paid, and social media.

- **Earned media** is generally free, meaning you don't pay monetarily for the placement, interview, or mention by a media outlet. If you engage a public or media relations firm or practitioner, you will pay fees for their work on your behalf. You should think beyond a media or news release. There are significantly more effective methods to engage journalists.

- **Owned media** includes publications, brochures, case studies, white papers, websites, opinion editorials, and other thought-leadership channels that you generate on behalf of your company. Again, placement of owned media is usually free. You will incur costs for editorial services if you engage a writer or editor or a communications professional for production, distribution, or placement.

- **Paid media** includes the advertisements, billboards, radio and broadcast commercials, point-of-sale displays, or other materials for which you purchase and control the message being communicated. While paid media is necessary in the marketing mix, it is not the most trusted information source for the increasingly skeptical and sophisticated consumer. For a greater return on your advertising investment, your paid media efforts must be coordinated and aligned with your earned, owned, and social media strategies.

- **Social media** involves engaging your customers, influencers, and others through electronic forms of communication to share information, experiences, and other content. Several of the most popular social media platforms for business include Facebook, Google+, LinkedIn, Twitter, and Pinterest. The most effective social media strategies actively and consistently engage their audiences on the platforms most relevant to their business goals, customer expectations, and brand voice.

Before engaging with the news media or launching an earned media program, you should consult with a public relations firm or practitioner or communications consultant. It is imperative that you understand the rules and protocols to engage with journalists. It also is highly recommended that you participate in a professional media training session.

Engaging with the media takes skill, expertise, and patience but can generate great awareness and visibility for you and your brand if executed correctly. But, when not properly executed, interacting with the media can damage your reputation and harm your brand.

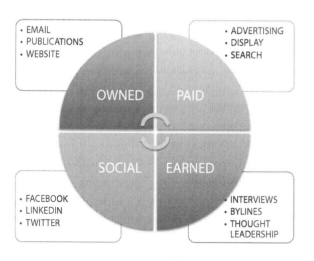

Harness your brand power

Figure 7

Employing an integrated communications strategy across your earned, owned, paid, and social media channels, enables you to rapidly build your brand, influence your reputation, and reinforce your brand promise through consistent, thoughtful, and compelling communication.

CHAPTER 11

Chop, Chop

"I had to make my own living and my own oppor-
tunity! But I made it! Don't sit down and wait for
the opportunities to come. Get up and make them!"
–Madam C.J. Walker

Here's where the proverbial rubber meets the road. With your assessments, road map, benchmarks, and strategies completed, you're ready to engage the professionals, your team, and employees to harness your brand power.

As I begin this chapter, I'm fully aware of the positive and significant impact your well-managed brand can have on your business and your future success. Quite often, I'm known for uttering this signature phrase: "chop, chop." For me, it simply means "do it now," as there is no time like the present to begin your brand journey.

And, your time is now. Your future awaits and you, your family, customers, and employees deserve nothing less. It's up to you to commit, engage, and execute a brand strategy that breaks your company out of the clutter.

You must engage your employees, customers, vendors, and professional consultants, as appropriate, to garner their guidance, input, and expertise. Harnessing your brand power takes your vision for and investment in your company to greater heights. It can provide significant opportunities while strategically managing the associated costs.

With nearly 30 years of experience creating and directing brand and reputation programs in the private, public, and nonprofit sectors, I know first-hand the significant impact a well-defined, professionally managed, and successfully communicated brand contributes to the profitability, sustainability, and longevity of large and, most important, small organizations.

Good luck on your journey, and best wishes for continued success. Chop, chop.

Appendix

Several assessment-, planning-, and strategy-development exercises, templates, and worksheets are available at

http://www.breakoutbrandstrategies.com.

For more information regarding our professional and coaching services or to request Renée for a seminar, workshop, facilitated executive session, keynote, or customized program, please send an e-mail to info@breakoutbrandstrategies.com, phone 888.270.7583 or visit

http://www.breakoutbrandstrategies.com.

Glossary

Breakout brand—a customer-centered, forward-focused, and imaginative perception existing in the minds of your customers, employees, and others that builds credibility, visibility, and a reputation for quality and that contributes to the organization's financial viability.

Dashboard—a visual display of the most important information needed to achieve one or more objectives, consolidated and arranged on a single screen so the information can be monitored at a glance.

Hobby business—an activity pursued without the expectation of making a profit. Losses experienced from a hobby are generally deductible only to the extent they can be used as an offset to hobby income.

Opportunity cost—a benefit, profit, or value of something that must be given up to acquire or achieve something else.

Strategist—a conceptual thinker who is able to use data and insight to undertake a long-range view, to align goals, and to plan resources and a course of action that achieve the desired goals and objectives.

Tactician—a person who provides planned support of programs or campaigns and deals with the implementation or execution of actions to resolve or address particular problems or opportunities.